Dance

Tap Dance

By Trudy Becker

level 2 little blue readers

www.littlebluehousebooks.com

Little Blue House is distributed by North Star Editions:
sales@northstareditions.com | 888-417-0195

Produced for Little Blue House by Red Line Editorial.

Photographs ©: iStockphoto, cover, 4, 7, 9, 10, 13, 15, 19, 21, 23, 24 (top left), 24 (bottom right); Shutterstock Images, 16, 24 (top right), 24 (bottom left)

Library of Congress Control Number: 2022919915

ISBN
978-1-64619-833-7 (hardcover)
978-1-64619-862-7 (paperback)
978-1-64619-917-4 (ebook pdf)
978-1-64619-891-7 (hosted ebook)

Printed in the United States of America
Mankato, MN
082023

About the Author

Trudy Becker lives in Minneapolis, Minnesota. She likes exploring new places and loves anything involving books.

Table of Contents

Click Clack

A girl dances on a stage. Her shoes click and clack on the hard floor.

A boy's arms reach out.
He spins, then clicks his feet again.
His moves are smooth and sharp.

A dancer's feet move
very fast.
Her shoes make sounds
on every touch.
She is tap dancing.

All About It

Tap dance is an
American dance.
It has parts of Irish and
West African dances.

Tap dancers have metal taps on their shoes. Taps make sounds when they hit the floor.

tap

Tap dancers move to music, but they also make music with their taps. The taps hit the floor again and again.

Learning How

Tap dancers use a hard floor
to practice.
The floor can make
sounds louder.

Tap dancers can wear fancy or plain outfits. They can wear pants or skirts.

outfit

Shoes are important.
Tap dancers need
tap shoes.
That is how they make
musical sounds.

tap shoe

Before showtime, tap dancers shake out their legs.

They click their shoes.

It is time to tap dance!

Glossary

hard floor

taps

practice

tap shoes

Index